DATE DUE

U.C. Library			
DEC 10 '88 U.C. Library			
GAYLORD			PRINTED IN U.S.A.

Headline Series

No. 275 **FOREIGN POLICY ASSOCIATION** $4.00

STRATEGIC DEFENSE INITIATIVE
Splendid Defense or Pipe Dream?

by Scott Armstrong and Peter Grier

1
Race for the High Ground   3

2
Cannons in Space   13

3
Battling with Beams   20

4
The Challenge of Mission Control   29

5
The Soviet Strategy   39

6
The Politics of Space   50

Talking It Over   59

Reprinted by permission from The Christian Science Monitor *© 1985 The Christian Science Publishing Society. All rights reserved. The articles appeared in November and December 1985. Mr. Armstrong wrote chapter 3, Mr. Grier wrote chapters 4 and 6; they collaborated on chapters 1, 2 and 5.*

Cover Design: Hersch Wartik

University of Charleston Library
Charleston, WV 25304

The Authors

SCOTT ARMSTRONG is a science and technology writer for *The Christian Science Monitor*. Before joining the *Monitor's* Science Page, Mr. Armstrong researched and wrote special section reports for the Business Page. A native of Oregon, Mr. Armstrong is a graduate of the University of Minnesota.

Photo by Paul W. Bailey Jr.

PETER GRIER has been a Washington bureau staff writer for *The Christian Science Monitor* since 1983. Prior to moving to Washington, D.C., in 1980, Mr. Grier was stationed in the *Monitor's* Boston headquarters where he worked in the New England news bureau, on special sections and as a radio news writer.

The Foreign Policy Association

The Foreign Policy Association is a private, nonprofit, nonpartisan educational organization. Its purpose is to stimulate wider interest and more effective participation in, and greater understanding of, world affairs among American citizens. Among its activities is the continuous publication, dating from 1935, of the HEADLINE SERIES. The authors are responsible for factual accuracy and for the views expressed. FPA itself takes no position on issues of United States foreign policy.

HEADLINE SERIES (ISSN 0017-8780) is published five times a year, January, March, May, September and November, by the Foreign Policy Association, Inc., 205 Lexington Ave., New York, N.Y. 10016. Chairman, Robert V. Lindsay; President, Archie E. Albright; Editor, Nancy L. Hoepli; Senior Editor, Ann R. Monjo; Associate Editor, K. M. Rohan. Subscription rates, $15.00 for 5 issues; $25.00 for 10 issues; $30.00 for 15 issues. Single copy price $4.00. Discount 25% on 10 to 99 copies; 30% on 100 to 499; 35% on 500 to 999; 40% on 1,000 or more. Payment must accompany order for $8 or less. Add $1 for postage. Second-class postage paid at New York, N.Y. POSTMASTER: Send address changes to HEADLINE SERIES, Foreign Policy Association, 205 Lexington Ave., New York, N.Y. 10016. Copyright 1986 by Foreign Policy Association, Inc. Composed and printed at Science Press, Ephrata, Pa.

Library of Congress Catalog Card No. 86-80312
ISBN 0-87124-103-X

Race for the High Ground

In the name of defending the nation, researchers in New Mexico have destroyed a missile carcass with a beam of light. In New Jersey, they have built an electric cannon that uses in a single burst as much current as the city of Newark. At a New York Air Force base, they are trying to develop electronic eyes sensitive enough to spot nicks on warheads in the vast dark of space. It's all part of what one researcher calls "splendid defense"—President Ronald Reagan's Strategic Defense Initiative (SDI), his vision of developing a screen to protect the United States from nuclear missile attack. Critics say it is a pipe dream, one that might precipitate, not prevent, Armageddon.

This issue of the HEADLINE SERIES will not try to decide between the judgments of "splendid defense" and "pipe dream." But it will explore the current state of technology of SDI and the options this now gives the United States in designing its multibillion-dollar program.

What began as a seemingly offhand remark by Mr. Reagan in a 1983 speech is evolving into one of the key global issues of our time. It proposes nothing less than a complete change in the way superpowers think about nuclear weapons. It is a central force shaping relations between the United States and the Soviet

Union. It perplexes, and at times peeves, America's European allies. It baffles Congress, divides scientists, and stirs the kind of passion in public more often associated with theological disputes.

"I think this offers more hope to the world than anything else," says Secretary of Defense Caspar W. Weinberger.

Scoffs IBM scientist Richard Garwin: It will require "a kind of magic spell that will turn warheads to dust."

The SDI, popularly known as "star wars," is not a search for a perfect defense. Disinvention of nuclear weapons is not possible. Neither can the United States turn itself into a giant domed stadium, the population safely inside.

SDI is instead a multibillion-dollar inquiry into the relative merits of imperfection. While a leakproof defense looks improbable, even critics concede that a screen could be built to stop some Soviet missiles. Thus the key questions related to technology and feasibility are: How well would such a system work? Could the United States afford it? What are the specific options?

A close look at the President's SDI program reveals these points:

• The next 18 months will be crucial for SDI. Members of Congress and lobbyists say they will devote full attention to the system for the first time. The Geneva arms talks may decide if SDI research proceeds full speed.

• Official SDI plans initially involve rockets, high-speed guns, and other kinetic-energy weapons, which depend on the energy of motion for their destructiveness. Lasers and other exotic beam weapons aren't expected to be added to the complex system until 2005 or 2010.

• Weapons will not be the hardest technical problem of star wars. That distinction will go to the computers, to communications, and to other support technologies needed to knit the weapons into an effective system.

• If SDI's goal is something less than perfection, it is also something more than mere protection of individual U.S. missile fields, the goal of earlier ballistic-missile defense programs.

• Technology alone can't make missiles obsolete. An effective defense of the U.S. population would probably require some cuts in Soviet offensive arms, say many SDI officials. This brings arms control into the picture.

● Cost is emerging as a major point of contention in the SDI debate. Administration officials concede they must be able to build a shield more cheaply than the Soviets can add offensive weapons to overwhelm it. Critics and supporters alike say this will be one of its toughest challenges.

Mr. Reagan's vision of a world bristling with defenses against nuclear arms is not a new idea. It's the latest phase of an on-again, off-again effort by the United States to build barricades against such arms—an effort dating back to the dawn of the Atomic Age. "There's such a sense of déjà vu to all this," says Gregg Herken, author of *Counsels of War,* a history of the nuclear age.

Early Defense Concepts

As early as the 1940s, atomic bomb pioneer J. Robert Oppenheimer urged the world to work on defense against his own creation, arguing it was a moral as well as strategic imperative. In 1958, startled by the Soviet launch of Sputnik, Secretary of Defense Neil McElroy ordered development of systems for shooting down incoming missiles. This led to Project Defender, a wide-ranging program that some analysts think was more ambitious for its time than SDI is today.

Many of Project Defender's ideas never went much beyond the chalkboard. One, Project HELMET, proposed planting giant howitzers near U.S. cities to shoot clouds of debris at incoming warheads. Another, SAMBO, called for orbiting a ring of pellets—in effect, an artificial asteroid belt—over known Soviet missile fields.

Other Project Defender work proved more enduring. Some of the earliest research on beam weapons occurred under the program, as did development of nuclear-tipped interceptor missiles. The latter became part of the only U.S. defense against nuclear arms ever deployed. It was installed in the 1970s to protect missile silos in North Dakota, but was later scrapped as too costly and ineffective.

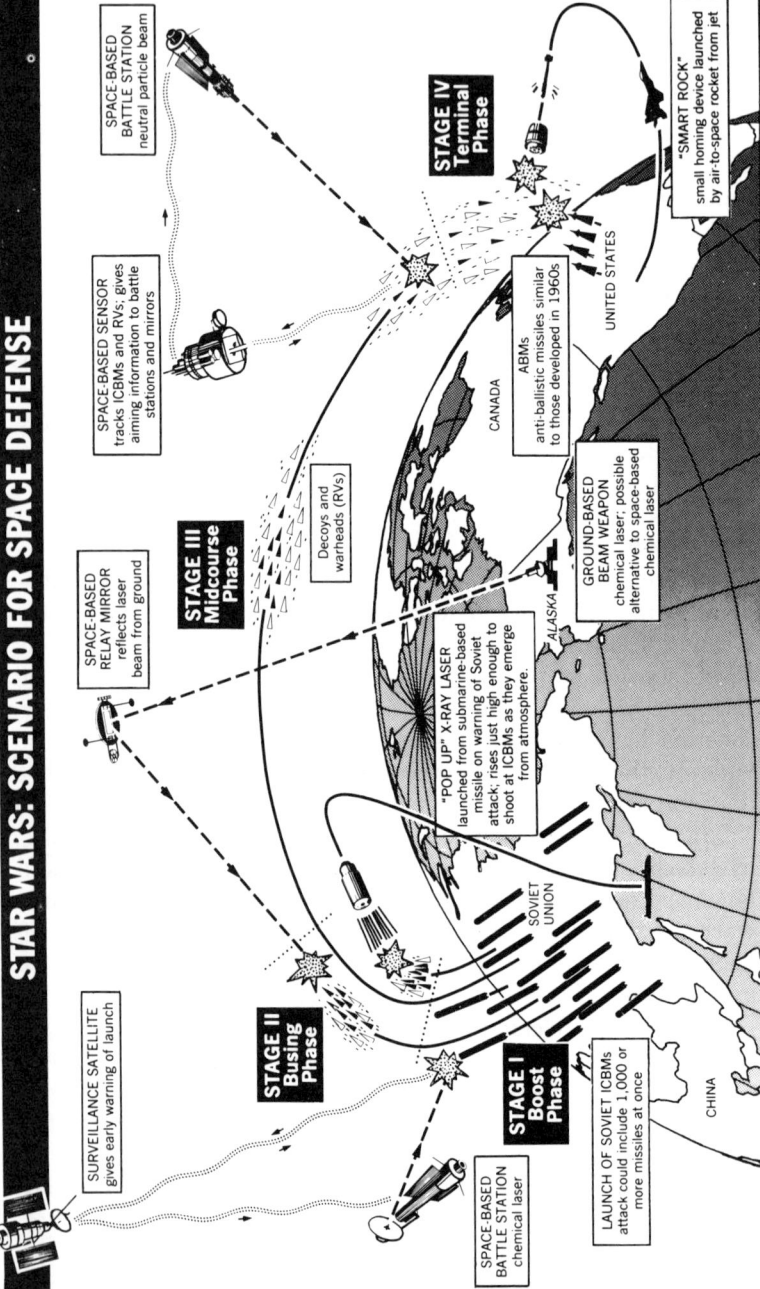

Reprinted with permission of *The Washington Post*.

In the end the United States decided that no defense against nuclear missiles was possible with the technology of the 1960s and '70s. The destructive force of nuclear weapons was so great that only something close to 100 percent defense would have any meaning. Even a few nuclear warheads that got through a screen would spell disaster. Offensive weapons had unchallenged technological primacy.

In 1972, the United States and the Soviet Union codified this mutual vulnerability in the Antiballistic Missile (ABM) Treaty, which prohibited development and deployment of nationwide ballistic-missile defenses. But the United States continued low-level research into missile-defense technologies. This work went almost unnoticed for years until March 23, 1983, when President Reagan's star-wars speech pulled it back into prominence.

On the surface, Mr. Reagan's speech seemed impulsive. In fact, it caught many of his closest aides by surprise. But underneath it seems to have reflected a variety of forces: technological advances that suggested an effective shield might for the first time be possible; Mr. Reagan's dissatisfaction, like that of presidents before him, with the uneasy balance of terror based on offensive arsenals; and personal appeals from advisers such as physicist Edward Teller, the father of the U.S. hydrogen bomb.

"The Soviets have a monopoly on defense," claims Dr. Teller.

The Layers of Defense

What sets the President's initiative apart from earlier thrusts is its stress on space components and a "layered" defense system. Previous efforts were mainly concerned with attacking warheads during their terminal phase, when the warheads reenter the atmosphere and dive toward targets.

Star-wars weapons would attack nuclear warheads at four phases of their 30-minute trip from silos to U.S. territory. First is the so-called boost phase, when a rocket rises through the atmosphere for three to five minutes. Next is post-boost, the three- to five-minute period when the warhead bus, which carries the guidance system, warheads, and decoys, separates from the booster and begins to cast off its warheads and decoys. Then comes midcourse, when warheads and thousands of decoys float through space for 15 to 20 minutes before reentering the atmosphere en route to their destructive destinations—the terminal phase.

In theory, each defensive layer could be somewhat leaky and still contribute to an effective shield. If each layer destroyed 75 percent of the warheads leaking through the preceding layer, only 4 out of every 1,000 Soviet warheads launched would detonate on U.S. territory.

To accomplish this task, a varied arsenal would probably be used, because not all weapons may be good for all uses. For example, kinetic-energy weapons may travel too slowly for use in the all-critical boost phase, when missiles are easy to find and warheads and decoys are wrapped in one neat package. Beam weapons can suffer similar limitations. For instance, some particle beams—which use streams of atoms or atomic particles accelerated to near the speed of light—can't penetrate the atmosphere. So they may not work for boost-phase duty. Certain lasers could eat down into the atmosphere, given much more brightness than they have now.

Under current SDI thinking, an initial missile screen would consist of "kinetic kill" weapons, such as quick rockets. If deployed at all, such a space-based defense would likely not come about before the mid-1990s. Exotic beam weapons would not be ready until the turn of the century.

Of course, it is not a foregone conclusion that these weapons will work. Most are now only lab experiments.

And any weapon, however powerful, is useless if it cannot be plugged into a working system. More than anything else, this is the requirement that makes star wars perhaps the most complex military undertaking ever.

The star-wars system first must find its targets. This would be particularly hard in the midcourse phase, when warheads and decoys may number a quarter of a million objects.

Picking out warheads from the radar-spoofing chaff, Mylar balloons, and other decoys will require new ways of getting different types of sensors to work together. "I think boost-phase intercept and midcourse discrimination are the key issues for a cost-effective defense," says Cornelius (Cory) Coll III, head of an SDI study group at Lawrence Livermore National Laboratory in Livermore, California.

Once targets are identified, weapons must be aimed and fired, and kills assessed. This requires ultra-fast communications and perhaps the most "intelligent" computers ever made. Computer hardware can probably be made to crunch numbers fast enough, though this will take plenty of work.

"It'll be like putting a Cray supercomputer on a sugar cube," says John Bosma, editor of the newsletter "Military Space." The computer he refers to can perform up to 1.2 billion calculations a second.

But writing the software—the instructions behind the number-crunching—may be the single most difficult task of the program. SDI officials say yet-unknown technological advances will help write the 10 million to 100 million lines of software needed.

Critics contend that software bugs could never be worked out of the system. "You'd have to have a real nuclear war to have operational testing," says David Redell, a Digital Equipment Corporation engineer.

Countering a Missile Defense

An even bigger concern: While the United States is developing defensive weapons, the Soviets will undoubtedly try to devise ways to counter them.

"Technology today is capable of shooting down offensive missiles. The question is: Can you do it in face of what the Soviets do in reaction?" says former Defense Secretary Robert S. McNamara.

The Kremlin might build more offensive missiles and warheads to try to saturate a defense. They might try disguises— balloons imitating warheads or warheads hiding in balloons. They might try to skirt a defense altogether by aiming submarine-launched ballistic missiles so they leave the atmosphere only briefly, if at all, or by developing ground-hugging cruise missiles and strategic bombers. These would be hard to zap from space.

But SDI advocates argue that some star-wars weapons may work against this threat, and that, in any case, it is important to blunt the accurate land-based ballistic missiles, the heart of the Soviet strategic arsenal.

Moscow could also design ways to foil specific defensive weapons. They could spin boosters like drill bits so that lasers can't dwell on one spot, or devise thick-skinned missiles to resist attack. Perhaps most worrisome, they could build fast-burn boosters that would complete their work while still in the atmosphere, hampering the ability of some weapons to reach them.

Fast-burn boosters would be costly, both in reducing the performance of a missile and on the Soviet economy—prohibitively so, SDI advocates say.

This type of measure-countermeasure gamesmanship will be expensive for both sides. "You want to make the Soviets spend a lot of money," says one SDI scientist.

Finally, the Soviets could simply punch a hole in a defense system. They might orbit "space mines" that would blow up on command and shower satellites with shrapnel. One SDI scientist worries about three other antidefense weapons: ground-based lasers; nuclear-tipped interceptor rockets; and X-ray lasers, beam weapons powered by small nuclear bombs. The United States is developing the X-ray laser as a possible defensive weapon, and the Soviets are known to be working on it as well.

"Many of these defensive technologies are the key to the destruction of the defense itself," Dr. Garwin says.

But battle stations may be able to defend themselves or have special "guard" satellites to do the job. They may be armored, or able to bob and weave when attackers approach.

"I worry about survivability. Along with cost, I see it as a major constraint to SDI," says Stephen Rockwood, head of SDI research at the Los Alamos National Laboratory in New Mexico.

Whatever its final capabilities, any defensive shield would be expensive—equal to adding another Navy to the budget, according to critic John E. Pike, space policy analyst of the Federation of American Scientists. Estimates of a star-wars system's cost run to $800 billion or more, but until the system takes shape such figures are guesswork at best.

What is known is that expenses would not stop with deployment. "Even in the absence of hostile action, there will have to be constant activity in space ... to maintain a working system," notes a report by Congress's Office of Technology Assessment.

Star wars, after all, would be unprecedented in scope. It requires advances in basic science and engineering, and must take into account a cunning adversary who can shoot back. Work on the program may span 20 to 30 years. By comparison, during World War II the Manhattan Project to develop the atomic bomb took four years; landing on the moon took eight.

Even if it turns out that a defensive shield can be built, and for something less than a year's gross national product, there's the more fundamental question of whether it should be built.

According to President Reagan, star wars is a way out of today's nuclear balance of terror, in which the superpowers refrain from war because each is able to retaliate against the other. The balance of terror resulting from the primacy of offensive nuclear weapons has dominated the four decades of the nuclear era; and the specific American doctrine of mutual assured destruction (MAD) has dominated U.S. military strategy for more than two decades.

SDI enthusiasts envision a world of "assured survival," in which the United States would once again control its own destiny. Under the most prevalent scenario, initial deployment of a defensive screen would deter the Soviets from launching a first strike because they would have doubts about how many of their missiles might get through. In effect, this would strengthen MAD, though not replace it.

Over time, the Soviets would come to see the futility of investing in offensive forces and would begin to reduce their arsenals, relying more on defense. The world would never become free of nuclear weapons. But their role would be greatly reduced. They would be unusable and hence obsolete, in the words of one Reagan official. "Obsolete and unusable, what's the difference?"

asks George A. Keyworth II, Mr. Reagan's science adviser. "This idea of needing an umbrella of perfection is misleading, because your real objective is to make nuclear weapons unusable."

Critics see more dangerous endings to this script. They are concerned that development of a U.S. shield will violate the 1972 ABM Treaty, unraveling the fragile fabric of arms control pacts. The response to U.S. defenses will be a Soviet arms buildup, they claim.

Even if the Soviets decide to set up their own version of SDI, the transition to a defense-oriented world would be tricky. If one side developed a superior defense, it might be able to strike first with its nuclear missiles, knowing that its shield was good enough to handle any retaliation. Thus defenses might heighten, rather than lessen, the chances of nuclear holocaust.

Another conundrum is what a defense-dominated world would mean for America's European allies. If a Soviet defense shield were deployed, Europe might once again be exposed to conventional war.

To the Reagan Administration, SDI is an example of technology leading diplomacy toward a safer world. To critics, the vision could do more harm than good. "It deludes the public into thinking that the solution to the dual problem of nuclear weapons and a troublesome adversary can be resolved by new weapons systems, rather than by political means," write Massachusetts Institute of Technology (MIT) professors George Rathjens and Jack Ruina.

Cannons in Space

It is the most powerful railgun in the world, and it now lies in pieces in a New Jersey Army lab. Using bursts of electricity instead of gunpowder, it shoots plastic cubes so fast that they carry the wallop of a Mack truck traveling 60 miles an hour. Someday, its descendants might blast missiles and warheads from the sky as if they were shooting skeet.

"We're talking about something that's really quite revolutionary," says Dr. Ted Gora, chief of railgun research at the Army's weapon design facility in Dover, N.J. Of the weapons the Pentagon is studying for use in ballistic-missile defense, lasers and other exotica have received the most public attention. But a star-wars system, at least at first, would likely rely on railgun projectiles and warheads on fast rockets. They get their destructiveness from kinetic energy, the energy of motion.

This kinetic-energy firepower is in essence high-technology artillery. It could be based on Earth or on platforms in space. In theory, it could attack enemy missiles at every stage—from the boost phase, when a missile is easiest to spot and all its warheads and decoys are in one neat package, to the terminal phase, when warheads are reentering the atmosphere. In practice, it might be difficult for projectiles to reach missiles during the all-crucial first few minutes of flight.

Some kinetic-energy weapons are technologically well developed. High-acceleration rockets, fired from the ground and intended to protect missile silos, are perhaps ready for deployment today. Others are still experimental. Railguns and other electromagnetic launchers excite many weapons designers, but power supplies for these devices pose problems, and the projectiles they shoot move so fast they tend to rip up the inside of the barrel.

"All of our experiments have not been raging successes," concedes Dr. Gora.

In Washington, SDI is an abstraction, budget figures on a page. The program's nickname—star wars—emphasizes its futuristic aura. But to Dr. Gora and others working on its technology, it is as real as the metal and wire in their labs.

Dr. Gora has been working on railguns for seven years in a shed-like building of the Army's Armament Research and Development Center. The Army has not always been wild about the project.

But Dr. Gora and cohorts—among them physicist Harry Fair, and William Weldon, now at the University of Texas (UT)—persevered. Now, with the coming of President Reagan's SDI program, railgun researchers are flush with money and respect. Enthusiasts say electric cannons could be the biggest jump in gun technology since the Chinese invented gunpowder in the ninth century.

This potential stems from the tremendous velocity reached by railgun projectiles. The destructive power of a bullet largely results from its mass and velocity: A small bullet traveling very fast can be the equal of a larger one that moves more slowly.

A bullet for an M-16 rifle travels just over 3,000 feet per second. In tests, the Army's New Jersey railgun has sent an 11-ounce plastic cube winging along at 2.6 miles per second. Other labs have shot small, thimble-sized objects at greater velocities (more than 6 miles per second). But the Army's railgun has hurled the largest projectile at high velocities. SDI officials envision a railgun that would shoot yet larger objects at up to 12 miles per second.

The Army railgun, never before seen by reporters, looks like 12 feet of large drainpipe with a cement mixer on one end. Inside the gun's barrel stretch two parallel copper rails.

When the gun is fired, a powerful electric current surges up one rail, hits the projectile, leaps across it to the other rail, and surges back toward the gun's breech. Contained by its own magnetic field, the electric force explodes forward, pushing the projectile as it goes.

Such brute force may have applications more terrestrial than shooting down missiles. The Army is interested in high-speed railgun artillery, which might be able to blast apart tanks as if they were made of balsa wood.

Harnessing the Power to Fire a Railgun

Electromagnetic launchers are not a new idea. At the turn of the century electrical engineers theorized that such guns were possible. During World War II, German scientists toyed with the technology—including using them to hurl cargo-laden gliders across battlefields. The Japanese tried to build an electric machine gun.

These efforts, say researchers, all foundered on the same problem: power. You could briefly light a large city with the pulse of electricity today's railgun experiments require. "Power supplies right now are larger and heavier than we would like them to be," says Mr. Weldon, director of the UT Center for Electromechanics.

But new advances hold hope that the problem of producing space-transportable, powerful generators can be solved, SDI officials say. For example, they point to a machine that Mr. Weldon perfected over the last decade. Called a compulsator, the device is capable of loosing huge surges of current in quick succession. This winter, UT researchers hope to fire a 10-shot burst with a compulsator-driven railgun. Last year, they successfully fired four projectiles in a row. Such machine-gun capability is crucial if railguns are to become viable missile-defense weapons.

Projectiles are another railgun problem. Electromagnetic launchers would be firing at targets hundreds of miles away. At such distances, shells must have some sort of ability to guide themselves to be accurate. They must be, in an oft-quoted phrase, smart rocks.

But current guidance technology—such as the heat-seeking sensors in air-to-air missiles—would be turned into silicon junk by the acceleration forces that railgun shells experience.

Tough new metal alloys and other materials would be needed for missile-defense railguns as well. Currently, railguns can be so scarred after one shot that their interiors must be rebuilt.

If railguns are to be put in space, they must also be made a fraction of their current size. The Army's New Jersey railgun experiment, with its support equipment, takes up one quarter of a room the size of a hangar. SDI officials ultimately envision a space-based weapon being something over 30 feet long and weighing around 40 tons.

"We need a jet aircraft to do the SDI job. We're at the propeller-plane stage now," says Gene McCall, a physicist at the Los Alamos National Laboratory in New Mexico.

Gazelle-Quick Rocket Interceptors

While railguns and other electromagnetic launchers are still experiments, another type of kinetic-energy weapon is much more technologically mature: lightning-quick rocket interceptors. The U.S. military now has a wide range of such rockets in its arsenal, from shoulder-fired, antiaircraft Stingers, to the Sidewinder, favored weapon of fighter pilots, and the recently tested Air Force antisatellite missile. This technology could be taken off the shelf, modified, and used to attack ballistic missiles and warheads in space, according to one view now gaining favor among SDI officials.

In this scenario, bundles of small rockets with explosive warheads would be mounted on satellites and sent into orbit. In times of political tension the satellite would be turned on alert and ordered to fire on ballistic missiles rising from the Soviet Union.

"The weapons could not kill people, because they would burn up before they got to the ground," claims Col. Malcolm O'Neill, head of SDI kinetic-energy weapon programs. "But they could kill anything flying in space, including missiles, reentry vehicles, or satellites."

This proposal for "porcupine" satellites mirrors a little-remembered 1960 Pentagon study named Project SPAD (Space Patrol Active Defense). SPAD recommended orbiting hundreds of small satellites, each studded with six small missiles, for defense against the burgeoning Soviet intercontinental ballistic missile (ICBM) force, according to Mr. Bosma, editor of "Military Space." The technology of the times was not up to the task, however, and Pentagon interest passed to other forms of antimissile systems.

Small space rockets must be cheap to build and orbit, SDI officials say, since they in theory will be fired in quantity at Soviet missiles.

They must also be able to reach their targets. This will be particularly hard in the critical boost phase—the three- to five-minute period between launch and the time when an ICBM's final booster stage burns out. Missiles are the most vulnerable during this phase: The engine exhaust is easy to spot and all the warheads are in one package.

If the Soviets adopted fast-burn boosters, which could take about 100 seconds to complete their work, the engines would burn out within the atmosphere. In either case, projectiles entering the atmosphere from the vacuum of space might break apart or generate enough heat to destroy their guidance systems.

Thus kinetic-energy weapons might not be quick enough to reach Soviet missile boosters before they burn out and release their warheads, a recent Congressional Office of Technology Assessment report points out.

Outside the atmosphere, rocket interceptors or railguns would have a relatively long time, 10 to 20 minutes, to reach targets. But these objects—small, dark warheads coasting through cold, dark space—would be extraordinarily difficult to find and track. SDI officials and critics alike rate this "midcourse discrimination" as one of the toughest technical problems the program faces.

The final option for kinetic-energy weapons would be to hit a warhead when it plunges back into the atmosphere and heads for its target. In this terminal phase, which lasts about a minute, kinetic weapons—probably rockets—would be based on the ground, and launched to intercept intruders. The United States fielded such a defense in the 1970s to protect missile silos in North Dakota. The Soviet Union has a similar defensive screen in place around Moscow.

These early defense systems, however, used nuclear-tipped interceptors. This time the Pentagon wants to use nonnuclear interceptor warheads.

Avoiding Nuclear-Tipped Interceptors

"What makes the terminal engagement so difficult is that we are going to do it without a nuclear weapon," says Colonel O'Neill. "My marching orders are that I have nothing nuclear."

Without the brute force of a nuclear explosion, rocket interceptors will have to be incredibly accurate. They will either have to collide with a warhead or get close enough to take it out with an explosion of shrapnel. Such accuracy has been demonstrated on a small scale.

In a much-publicized experiment in June 1984, the Army used a rocket interceptor to catch a dummy warhead over the Pacific. Ground-based radar and the interceptor's sensors were used to zero in on the device. Then the interceptor unfurled a metal umbrella and destroyed the warhead.

In a nuclear war, however, there would likely be hundreds of warheads falling on the United States that would have to be found and foiled. Special radar and sensing systems will be needed—systems that would also have to be resistant to blinding by nuclear explosions. Such blasts would result if an attacker sets warheads to explode when an interceptor comes too close.

Interceptor rockets, too, would have to be fast enough to stop warheads high in the atmosphere, so that if the warheads went off they wouldn't harm people on the ground. Colonel O'Neill says this will take "incredibly hot rockets," perhaps capable of reaching their targets within 10 seconds.

It is clear that in the not-too-distant future kinetic-energy weapons will be capable of knocking down some targets during a nuclear attack. The question is: How expensive and effective would such a defense be?

A first-step missile defense deployed in this century, say SDI officials, would likely rely heavily on kinetic-energy weapons, with more exotic stuff such as lasers used for target tracking and communication. But to build a final shield highly effective against attack and all countermeasures, directed-energy weapons—an even more difficult frontier—are necessary.

Battling with Beams

About a dozen people, mainly military brass, were crowded into a control bunker three stories beneath the New Mexico desert at the White Sands Missile Range. Peering anxiously at a bank of monitors and computer screens, they watched as a laser beam the diameter of a Hula-Hoop flashed a half-mile across the desert floor, glanced off a focusing mirror, and lit on a section of a Titan missile. Seconds later, the rocket stage suddenly blew up, scattering shards of metal hundreds of feet amid the mesquite and piñon.

"I've been in this business for 12 years," says Capt. Arthur Schroeder, head of the Navy's work at White Sands, who watched the demonstration in September 1985. "It was the most dramatic damage and vulnerability test I've ever seen."

Impressive as it was, it does not prove that lasers can be used to defend the United States against nuclear annihilation. The test was simply one more small step in a long and arduous quest to see if directed-energy, or beam, weapons ever may be suitable for knocking down Soviet missiles.

Beam weapons are gaining prominence. Once confined to science fiction, these "death rays" consist mainly of particle beams, which hurl streams of atoms or atomic particles, and lasers. These technologies have been elevated to new visibility under President Reagan's SDI.

Indeed, they are one of the reasons that the United States has revived the idea of building defenses against ICBMs after scotching it in the 1970s.

Earlier it was thought that there was no way to deal with tens of thousands of warheads and decoys that might be launched against the United States in a full-scale nuclear assault. There still may not be.

But a defender's job would be easier if a system could knock out as many missiles as possible within the first few minutes of launching, before they had a chance to release their many decoys and warheads. Beam weapons flashing through space at or near the speed of light are prime candidates for the job.

Conceptually, they make captivating weapons: beams of pinpoint precision able to zap mankind's most destructive armament. But translating that vision into reality will be difficult.

Physicists have been toiling for more than a quarter of a century to fashion directed-energy weapons, as they are called. The Pentagon launched its first particle-beam research program, the Seasaw project, in 1958 at Lawrence Livermore National Laboratory. The aim: to build a particle-beam accelerator and study its potential for thwarting missiles.

Interest in laser weapons surfaced shortly after that. In the years since, enthusiasm for these exotic weapons has vacillated. Hopes raised by advances in technology were often dashed when people began to look at the cost and other problems tied to building a practical weapons system.

The military is still keen on beam weapons for everything from air defense to destroying enemy satellites. The SDI program, however, focuses attention on the far more difficult task of destroying enemy missiles and warheads, for which $1 billion is being sought in 1986 alone (about one fourth the SDI budget).

Given the hurdles that remain, particularly the defensive tricks the Soviets may try (such as spinning a booster so a laser cannot dwell on one spot), even SDI officials do not see a practical and affordable beam-weapon system this century. Divining what the Soviets might do is like a chess game, says Louis Marquet, head of SDI's directed-energy programs. "Unfortunately, the Soviets are very good at chess."

Infrared Chemical Lasers

Light from a normal lamp is a disorderly jumble of frequencies. Lasers generate concentrated beams of light that are almost perfectly parallel, identical in frequency, and the light waves move in phase with each other. This gives lasers their punch. In theory, they could be focused over thousands of miles of space to burn a hole in the skin of a missile or, in the case of lasers that emit pulses, thump the target like a sledgehammer.

The most powerful lasers now in existence are chemical. They draw their energy from the combustion of gases. Because they do not require huge power plants, chemical lasers are mainly being considered for parking in space, where they would be free from the distorting effects of the earth's atmosphere.

These lasers pack a punch. Ones far less powerful than that tested here at White Sands—a 2.2-megawatt device that is the "brightest" in the West—have already knocked down planes. But space-weapons lasers will have to be brighter (probably 10 times or more).

Such infrared chemical lasers also have a long wavelength. Because their beams spread out over great distances, they would need to linger on the same spot on a fast-moving missile for several seconds. They also would require exquisitely fabricated mirrors of up to 50 feet in diameter to keep them focused. This has caused them to fall from grace with some in the SDI community.

Any orbiting constellation of chemical-laser battle stations will have to meet several criteria: be reliable, be cheap enough to hoist into orbit and maintain, and be able to survive a direct attack—for instance, from exploding satellites (space mines) the Soviets may park next to the weapons platforms.

"The difference between putting something up in space that can fire once or twice and something that will keep missiles from landing on top of you is a big one," says Jeff Hecht, author of the widely respected book *Beam Weapons*.

Free-Electron and Excimer Lasers

The alternative is to use shorter-wavelength lasers, such as the free-electron and excimer lasers. These are now the fair-haired beams among SDI researchers. A free-electron laser uses a huge particle accelerator to generate the electrons that, when passed through a series of wiggling magnets, are the source of the device's ultraviolet light.

These lasers have been developing the quickest. "They've come along in not many years from a scientific curiosity to reality," says Gerald Yonas, SDI's chief scientist.

In theory, free-electron lasers can be tuned to different wavelengths to allow their beams to slip through Earth's atmosphere. They also can be scaled to large powers and operated at high efficiencies. But for now, they exist only in early-stage laboratory models. Because the free-electron laser's accelerator requires a jumbo power source, it is a better bet for basing on the ground.

Prodigious electrical requirements are likely to keep the excimer earthbound as well. The excimer does not require a particle accelerator, but it does use a lot of power in producing an ultraviolet beam from rare gases.

Ground-basing is not necessarily a woe. It makes the complex devices simpler to tinker with, easier to defend, and, as Dr. Marquet likes to point out, "You could plug them into Hoover Dam, turn off the lights when the war starts, and deliver all the electricity into the devices." Which you may have to do: By one estimate, powering enough of these lasers to hit 2,000 targets may gobble up as much energy in a few minutes as New York City uses in several hours.

One scheme calls for placing the lasers on mountaintops and firing them high into space, where their beams bounce off huge relay mirrors and then off smaller aiming mirrors in lower orbits. Or the beams might simply be bounced off of "catch and transmit" mirrors in low-earth orbit. Either way, these devices will need mirrors of gemlike quality, larger than any built to date.

To meet this requirement, scientists are considering using mirrors made up of many small segments, like a mosaic, all computer controlled. The same general principle (adaptive optics) is aiding scientists in overcoming another problem with ground-based lasers: atmospheric distortion. So far, however, experiments have only been carried out with low-power beams.

The other snag with short-wavelength lasers is that they can be self-destructive. An excimer laser may be able to disable a booster in two seconds, which would negate the effect of spinning it to counteract the beam. But the excimer could also buckle its own mirrors.

New mirror coatings are being developed, but this is considered one of the more intractable SDI technologies. At a conference in the spring of 1985, James Stanford of the Naval Weapons Center in California noted that only 2 percent of the coatings now available meet even currently known requirements.

Pop-up X-ray Lasers

Of course, defenders could alleviate many of the problems with ground- or space-based systems by simply popping lasers into orbit at the first hint of a Soviet strike. This is where the nuclear-pumped X-ray laser comes in. This weapon appears to be advancing technically but losing ground politically.

The idea sounds simple: Explode a nuclear bomb in a small chamber ringed with rods and pointed at a target. When the explosion's radiant energy hits the rods, it produces a pulse of highly lethal X-rays, spraying them out in the instant before the device vaporizes.

But there are snags. Even though work on the secret devices at Lawrence Livermore has been moving quickly, scientists still have to invent more efficient "third generation" nuclear devices that will convert more of their energy into X-rays instead of explosions. Researchers will also have to control and aim the pulses to hit quick-moving targets.

X-ray lasers, too, have put the Reagan Administration in the uncomfortable position of pursuing a weapon driven by a nuclear bomb (albeit theoretically a small one) to help make nuclear weapons "obsolete." In theory, hundreds of such lasers could be orbited. But SDI officials now go to great pains to say that will not be done.

The pop-up scheme involves putting X-ray lasers atop missiles safely stored beneath the sea on submarines or on land-based launchers and lofting them into space at the first sign of a Soviet strike—the pet idea of Dr. Teller, an inveterate SDI booster.

To get the weapons into space quickly enough, however, they would require extremely fast launchers and perhaps the submarines would have to be parked vulnerably close to Soviet shores.

"The practicality of a global scheme involving pop-up X-ray lasers of this type is doubtful," said a recent Congressional Office of Technology Assessment study.

X-rays also do not penetrate Earth's atmosphere well. Thus if the Soviets were to use "fast-burn" boosters—which would complete their flight within 100 seconds, while still in the atmosphere—the weapon might not be effective for knocking out ICBMs in the all-critical boost phase, when warheads and decoys are in one package and the missile is easy to detect. Currently, the boost phase lasts from three to five minutes.

Lawrence Livermore scientists are not ready to concede lasers cannot be made bright enough to eat part way into the atmosphere. "It doesn't violate any laws of physics to do so," says George Miller, deputy associate director for nuclear design.

But X-ray lasers are considered more likely for post-boost duty, when the missile is just beginning to cast off its warheads and is still somewhat easy to find.

In addition, the X-ray lasers could be used during the midcourse phase, when the warheads and swarms of decoys are floating through space. However, because the X-ray laser is basically a one-shot device, some critics think it will be able to wipe out only a limited number of decoys and warheads.

The chief concern, however, seems to be that detonating a series of nuclear bombs in space might damage America's own battle stations and satellites. This point bothers even many in the SDI community.

"I don't find it to be a credible weapons system, even if it does work," says Dr. Rockwood, head of SDI work at Los Alamos.

X-ray-laser proponents say they believe battle stations could be hardened against the effects of nuclear explosions. They also say the device holds such potential, either as a defensive weapon or one to take out Soviet satellites, that the United States can't afford to give up studying it.

High Cost of Space Transport

The particle beam—a stream of atomic particles or atoms—is the Hercules of directed-energy weapons: It comes in a large package and packs a potent punch. The beam penetrates a missile's skin and destroys the insides, unlike most lasers, which deposit their energy on the surface.

This means particle beams could disable a target quickly. It also means they would be tough for Soviet scientists to foil, either by shielding the missile or spinning it. The particle beam's penetrating character, however, has its drawbacks: Because the beam immobilizes the internal electronics, it might take some time to verify that a target had been destroyed or disabled. Thus a particle-beam weapon may continue to fire at a target long after it had actually been "killed." In the meantime, other warheads race past.

The most likely candidate for a missile-zapper would be a neutral-particle beam, which, because it can't penetrate the atmosphere, would have to be parked in space. The particle beam's bulk is not endearing. Scientists figure a neutral-beam battle station might be 80 feet long and weigh 50 to 100 tons (the space shuttle carries 33 tons). Up to 100 may be required. "The problem for particle beams is one of packaging and engineering," says Dr. Rockwood. "They will have to be compact, lightweight, and fully remote controlled."

Blunted by Earth's atmosphere, neutral-particle beams would be of little use for boost-phase kills. But they look more suitable for post-boost and midcourse phases.

One type of charged-particle beam—the electron beam—can

operate in the atmosphere. Indeed, it has to: Its interaction with the surrounding atmosphere helps hold it together. If shot in space, the beam would almost immediately disperse as its electrons repelled each other. Even if the electrons remained in a narrow stream, it would be bent uncontrollably by Earth's magnetic field (neutral beams are immune to such mischief). Thus, the electron beam is being looked at for use on the ground to zap warheads dropping from space. The idea would be to use them to defend ships or U.S. missile silos and command posts.

The perfect weapon? Not quite. As yet, researchers have only been able to control the beams over very short distances in the atmosphere. One possible solution: Use a laser to "tunnel" a path for the particle beam through the air. Scientists at Sandia National Laboratory in New Mexico have tested this technique in a special gas-filled chamber. For now, however, the trick looks more like a coup for science than anything to make the Soviets nervous: The gas used in the tests doesn't exist in Earth's atmosphere.

At Lawrence Livermore, meanwhile, researchers are enthusiastic about work they are doing with the Advanced Test Accelerator, a device nearly the length of a football field bunkered in the flaxen hills east of San Francisco. With something greater than the sound of cracking helmets, it propels pulses of electrons up to 50 million electron-volts of energy—in effect creating synthetic lightning.

When technicians fire the beam into the air for the first time within the next several months, they're hoping to keep it controlled for some 75 feet—something that would be a leap forward but would still fall shy of the several miles that will be needed for a weapon. "You're talking about a long row to hoe," says physicist William Barletta, head of the beam research program at Lawrence Livermore. "We're still working on the basic physics."

If and when scientists work out the physics, they'll also have to be mindful of the cost. "For terminal defense, if we can't keep the costs down to $100 [million] to $200 million a copy, it won't be worth looking at," says Dr. Barletta.

Beyond this, star-wars officials are exploring even more-exotic concepts to thwart missiles, though most of these ideas are not much more than theories now. Two examples: gamma-ray lasers and "plasmoids."

Like the X-ray laser, gamma-ray lasers would be pumped by a nuclear bomb. Because gamma rays are more lethal than X-rays, one SDI booster says such a device would be the "ultimate directed-energy weapon."

Plasmoids are clouds of energized atomic nuclei and electrons that scientists would like to hurl at warheads. But first they will have to find a way to make the cloud stick together in space.

Given the work to be done, it's perhaps not surprising that beam weapons in general are not envisioned as part of a first-generation defense.

Their first role would probably be a supporting one—doing such things as helping discriminate decoys from warheads.

Even if space weapons can be built, they will have to be knit together in a reliable system. Most experts agree that developing technologies to run the battle will be far harder than developing the weapons.

The Challenge of Mission Control

If a star-wars control room is ever built, it may resemble the secure Air Force lab at Griffiss Air Force Base, N.Y. The lights are soft, the walls sound-absorbing, and the computers look like a new generation of video game.

In a nuclear attack, such a center would have to watch thousands of objects: missile boosters, warheads in space, strips of foil chaff, decoy balloons. Still-unknown electronics would handle the task; today's technology, fast as it is, would simply crash.

Designing this battle-management equipment will be "horrendous," says one scientist. And it is such mundane-sounding problems that may determine the viability of ballistic missile defenses.

Lasers of gigawatt [1 million kilowatts] power and railguns are impressive technology. But if no control system tells them what to do, space-based weapons are nothing but man-made asteroids wearing American flags.

SDI officials say the highest technical obstacles to missile defense include:

• Computers. Computing hardware powerful enough to run a space defense now seems feasible, but scientists aren't sure if they can write the programs—or software—needed to make the hardware run.

● Command and control. The various parts of a missile defense must be able to talk back and forth and work together, even in the face of massive attack.

● Target spotting. A missile roaring out of a silo is as easy to see as a 10-story burning building, but cold warheads coasting through space are extremely difficult for sensors to "discriminate."

● Power. A space-based weapon platform might require the energy of "10 Hoover Dams in one second," says "Military Space" editor Bosma.

● Transportation. The cost of putting things in orbit must be reduced 90 percent if space-based defense is to be affordable.

The men and women working on SDI say their job is to stand up sometime near the turn of the decade and say of these problems: "Yes, we think they can be solved," or "No, it's beyond us. Sorry." To make that decision, they must have some idea of what the entire missile defense might look like—a task taking much of their attention right now.

In essence, SDI's system is being shaped by a brainstorming competition. Last year, 10 teams of companies won contracts to draw up an SDI "architecture," or overall plan. This summer, companies such as Martin Marietta, TRW, and Boeing were picked to polish their plans more, in the competition's second phase.

Those who've seen the closely held studies say three schemes for an initial missile defense system are emerging.

The first is multilayered, using weapons such as homing rockets on platforms in space and on the ground.

The second is less ambitious, featuring ground-based rockets and surveillance sensors that would be popped into space on notice of attack.

The third is a completely ground-based defense intended to protect Europe against intermediate-range nuclear missiles such as the Soviet SS-20.

None of these initial plans involves lasers or particle beams to shoot things down. Research in these exotic technologies has given the SDI program an otherworldly sheen and helped earn it the nickname star wars, but directed-energy weapons are still more prospect than fact.

Lasers and particle beams might be added to a defensive system after initial deployment, say SDI officials, particularly if the Soviets keep building new missiles. Eventually, the United States might field a complex screen with directed-energy beams, kinetic-kill weapons, and as many as seven layers, according to SDI plans.

"It may be necessary to have directed-energy technology available in 2005, or 2010," says Navy Comdr. James Offut, with the SDI systems office.

The design of the SDI system is still evolving—the company studies are more plans to make plans than plans in themselves. But it's clear that SDI is considering defenses more limited than a complex umbrella intended to be 90 percent effective.

"You can contribute to deterrence, to stability in the strategic sense, by constructing defenses less than thoroughly reliable," says Commander Offut.

The Need for Stalwart Computers

For any U.S. missile shield to be at all reliable it must have stalwart computers. And the computers must be fast—so fast they would be to today's technology what an F-16 is to a biplane.

The Pentagon is counting on new semiconductor-chip design and new ways of linking computers together to provide this raw processing power. Even critics say these approaches hold promise.

"The hardware program is not insurmountable," says John Kogut, a University of Illinois physicist who opposes SDI.

But teaching these speedy computers to operate is another matter. Mr. Kogut and other critics claim that software poses unsolvable problems for ballistic missile defense.

Everyone involved agrees that writing SDI's software would be a monumental task, the data-processing equivalent of building the Great Pyramids of Giza. A ballistic missile defense would

Strategic Defense
Here are some of the more commonly heard

Proponents' case:	Opponents argue:	Proponents reply:
1. A defensive shield will make nuclear weapons obsolete.	Because a star-wars system can't be perfect, it won't remove the threat of nuclear war entirely.	You don't need perfection. With even a limited defense, an opponent wouldn't know how many of his warheads will get through, so he'd be less likely to strike first. If he does strike first, a defense would preserve more of the U.S. retaliatory force.
2. Because SDI-type defenses would thwart the use of ICBMs, it will lead the United States and the U.S.S.R. to reduce voluntarily their nuclear arsenals.	One way to beat a defense is to build more missiles to overwhelm it. This would lead to violations of arms treaties. So would testing and deployment of SDI-type weapons. All of this would pull the rug out from under the arms control process.	Deterrence is still shaky, despite arms control treaties. Look at how nuclear arsenals have grown since World War II.
3. SDI-type defenses could neutralize accidental or unauthorized launches or attacks by terrorists or other third parties.	There are cheaper ways to prevent accidents. Put command-destruct devices on missiles to destroy them if they're launched accidentally. As for terrorists, they're more likely to deliver a bomb in a suitcase or car trunk than on an ICBM.	Any system that can reduce the number of casualties is worth building.
4. SDI would enhance deterrence by helping U.S. retaliatory forces survive a nuclear attack. This would discourage Soviet leaders from launching a first strike.	But SDI might give the United States confidence to strike first in a crisis. After all, it's easier for an imperfect defense to counter a ragged response than a coordinated first strike.	This is a defensive system; it is not designed to make aggression easier. Besides, when the United States had clear nuclear superiority it didn't engage in nuclear blackmail.
5. SDI would help protect U.S. allies in Europe against nuclear attack.	Maybe so, but it then leaves Western Europe open to *conventional* attack.	Conventional war is preferable to nuclear war—especially since conventional weapons can be recalled.
6. SDI takes advantage of the U.S. technological lead over the Soviets.	That doesn't mean the Soviets won't respond. Since World War II, they've matched many U.S. weapons developments.	A high-tech race works to the U.S.'s advantage: If the Soviets copy U.S. technology, the United States will be ahead in the race.
7. Technological spinoffs from SDI will help the rest of the U.S. military and even find civilian uses.	The classified status of most SDI research will prevent quick use of spinoff technology. SDI may draw research money and manpower away from civilian work. It would be better just to spend the money for commercial R&D.	There are plenty of examples of commercial technology that came from classified military programs. Take a look at jet engines and nuclear power.

Initiative Debate
arguments for and against President Reagan's SDI.

Opponents' case:	Proponents argue:	Opponents reply:
1. SDI threatens to base weapons in space.	SDI offers a chance to negotiate treaties that nearly eliminate nuclear weapons.	The arms race wouldn't end: One way to counter a defense is to build more missiles. In fact you'd add two *more* races: one over defensive weapons and one over countermeasures.
2. SDI will undermine the ABM Treaty, which presumes that if there are no defenses the strategic balance will be more stable.	You assume a defense is deployed. SDI is a *research* program being conducted within the limits of the ABM Treaty. Besides, the Soviets have their own star-wars program.	SDI may be research, but some of the demonstrations planned involve devices that could be seen as "components" under the ABM Treaty, hence testing them would be a violation.
3. Even if 95 percent effective—much higher than current estimates—a defense system will allow enough warheads to get through to inflict untold damage on the American society.	Without defenses, all of the warheads in a Soviet first strike could hit the United States, destroying our ability to retaliate.	We can retaliate using submarine-based missiles. Even if a defense stops some Soviet warheads, it would still let enough through to destroy the United States as a nation.
4. A star-wars system will be destabilizing because its orbiting weapons will be vulnerable to attack and because the Soviets could build more offensive weapons to overwhelm it.	One object of SDI is to make it so expensive for the Soviets to overwhelm it that they give up that option. And because this reduces the utility of nuclear weapons, the Soviets should be more willing to negotiate arms reductions.	Possible countermeasures are numerous. They're already being explored by the United States and the Soviets. While we put weapons into orbit, they'll put countermeasures on a new generation of ICBMs.
5. The United States will have to convince the Soviets that relying on ballistic-missile defenses is better than relying on the doctrine of mutually assured destruction.	The Soviets have always placed a high value on defenses, even if they're marginal. SDI merely shows that the United States values defense, too.	True, the Soviets value defense: They are beefing up their air defense screen. But that doesn't mean it will be easy to talk them out of the ABM Treaty.
6. America's allies are concerned that SDI will speed the arms race between the United States and the U.S.S.R.	Perhaps. But the Europeans are also intrigued by the possibility that getting a share of the SDI pie will help their high-tech industries.	Given our efforts to halt the transfer of militarily sensitive technology, allied participation is likely to be quite limited.
7. The cost of a star-wars system is likely to be prohibitive.	Cost estimates at this point are flaky. There is no clearly defined system on which to base them. Besides, Reagan Administration officials have said that if research shows that a cost-effective defense can't be designed, it won't be pursued.	We *do* have spending targets for the SDI research program: $26 billion by 1990. So much will have been spent by that time that the program will become self-perpetuating, even if it proves infeasible to deploy a defense.

Lisa Remillard in *The Christian Science Monitor* © 1985 TCSPS.

need from 10 million to 100 million lines of software code that would tolerate faults—"understand what is a hiccup, and fix it," in the words of Commander Offut.

Judgments of whether the job can be done at all depend crucially on new technology. To scientists working on SDI, a coming generation of software whiz kids will use new computer technologies, such as artificial intelligence (AI), which tries to duplicate an expert's thought process in software, to perfect strategic-defense computer programs. "Artificial intelligence has had a lot of hype, but its applicability is real," says Ray Urtz, a technical director at the U.S. Air Force's Rome, N.Y., Air Development Center.

Air Force researchers using AI, for instance, are now developing a computer program that would help pilots pick the safest route through antiaircraft defenses to a target.

To critics, AI is akin to nuclear fusion power—technology that marches bravely onward, but never seems to get anywhere. In addition, they claim that SDI software could never be fully tested without war, and therefore would not be trustworthy.

And some engineers say missile-defense programs would inevitably be full of conceptual errors; humans cannot foresee and write in computer code all the things that might happen in a nuclear attack.

"Sometime in my lifetime I might see something like this, but I'm skeptical," says Dr. Redell of the Digital Equipment Corporation's Systems Research Center.

Missile-defense electronics running at full speed would have to keep an eye on all hostile missiles, warheads, and decoys; send orders to defensive weapons about what to shoot; and evaluate battle progress. To help this command-and-control process run smoothly, SDI scientists are trying to give the system's front-line "soldiers" as much responsibility as possible.

Surveillance satellites, for instance, might have powerful signal processors on board so they can process their own raw data. There might be "lieutenant-general" computers in orbit, each capable of running the battle in its area of the front. "That way, the enemy has to take out lots of things to wreck the system," says

Dr. Charles Johnson, IBM director of battle-management architectures.

Who Is Going to Run the System?

But SDI officials are not sure who, or what, might serve as a missile-defense commander in chief.

The problem is that a missile-defense system must have the reflexes of a soccer goalie. Its success might hinge on destroying ICBMs during their boost phase, which currently takes about three to five minutes. That does not allow much time to call the President in from a golf course.

So a U.S. space shield would probably be controlled by an on-duty, high-ranking military officer, who would watch over a highly automated system, say SDI officials. Such delegation of authority is permissible, they say, because a missile-defense system would likely not use nuclear weapons; set off by accident, defensive weapons would sparkle harmlessly in space.

"Although it might alarm the world, the consequences of a mistake are minimal," says Dino Lorenzini, head of SDI's pilot architecture program.

Advancing technology might at some point bring the President and other civilian leaders in on missile-defense decisions, claims Mr. Lorenzini. "They may have a little electronic gadget embedded in their ear at all times," he says.

Advances in many technologies will be needed if missile defense is to prove feasible. Lasers, computers, and communications are just a few of them. But one of the toughest technical problems, say many scientists, is an obscure one—target spotting, or discrimination.

To see a rocket roaring up in boost phase all you need are binoculars and a fairly close seat. The trouble starts when the rocket burns out, and thousands of cold, dark warheads separate and coast across cold, dark space.

Critics, such as Richard Garwin, say that in this obscurity no electronic eye could reliably tell nuclear reentry vehicles from clever decoys. Military researchers are more optimistic.

"Finding them will require a multisensor approach," says

Frank Rehn, a technical director at Rome Air Development Center. Space-based radar might locate objects coming up through the clouds. Huge arrays of infrared detectors might pick up the trail, and lasers might push the objects, determining if they are warheads or lightweight balloons.

Much of the work on missile-defense sensors might be applied to other military missions. The Air Force, for instance, wants to use space-based radar to detect cruise missiles. Today's experimental Stealth airplanes, intended to be almost invisible to current radar, might well look big as blimps to sensors developed by SDI work, according to scientists in and outside of government.

These fancy new surveillance eyes in the sky would require large amounts of electric power. In fact, generating power in orbit is a key problem facing SDI researchers. Around the SDI office, officials joke privately about running extension cords up into space.

Big battle-management satellites might need 75 kilowatts of power—about as much as Skylab produced, says an SDI official. But the vast expanse of solar panels that Skylab used would be vulnerable in the heat of battle.

Exotic-weapons platforms would need even more electric power. Electromagnetic railguns might use short bursts of 1 gigawatt; some types of lasers might need bursts in the 40-gigawatt range.

Among the power technologies SDI is looking at are chemically powered generators, advanced batteries, and small, orbiting nuclear reactors. The National Aeronautics and Space Administration, the Department of Energy and the SDI organization are working on the SP-100, a space reactor that might produce up to 2 megawatts.

"Even without SDI, this nation will have to face the political reality of accepting space nuclear power," says Air Force Col. George Hess, director of SDI's program in survivability, lethality and key technologies.

It seems that any robust missile defense would inevitably count on some large components in space. They may be nuclear reactors and lasers; they may simply be large banks of infrared "eyes." Somehow, these things would have to be sent into orbit, and that is yet another large problem.

High Cost of Space Transport

It's a problem because currently transporting an object into space costs more than plating it with gold. The launch price for a satellite now hovers around $1,400 a pound. Unless that can be cut to $140 a pound or less, a space-based missile defense would probably be too expensive, SDI officials say.

As far as SDI is concerned, the space shuttle is only a pickup truck—it can carry about 30 metric tons. The Fletcher panel, a Reagan-appointed group, headed by James C. Fletcher, which studied missile-defense technologies, concluded that SDI needs a fleet of big rockets able to boost 100 metric tons into low-Earth orbit and beyond.

In addition "there are some advanced ideas for vehicles that take off from runways and then go supersonic [into orbit]," says Dr. Yonas, SDI chief scientist. "Those advanced ideas will come along in the fullness of time."

The issue of cost, evidenced in the problem of space transport, hangs over the whole SDI program. Reagan Administration officials have said that they would not favor deployment of a ballistic missile defense unless it is cheaper for the United States to strengthen its shield than it is for the Soviets to increase their offensive forces.

Even if that condition is met, the overall price of the shield could still give Congress sticker shock. As a recent Congressional Office of Technology Assessment report notes, "the cost and effort of a space-based [defense] does not end with deployment. Even in the absence of hostile action, there will have to be constant activity in space, occasionally with human presence, to maintain a working system."

Would the system survive an attack? SDI officials say that might depend on a combination of things, such as physical shielding of space systems and tactics (satellites that dodge, perhaps).

"With a lot of Yankee ingenuity, I think we could build the lasers, build the particle beams to the required standards," says Mr. Coll, leader of an SDI study group at Lawrence Livermore. "But this defensive system is more than a sum of its parts."

If I walked into a garage and saw all these beautiful automobile parts, I wouldn't know when I put them all together if I was going to get a Mercedes or an Edsel. I think putting this together in a system is going to be the major challenge."

The Soviet Strategy

The Soviet response to America's "Star Wars" could be called "The Empire Strikes Back." It would be a sequel every bit as important as the first installment, for Moscow's actions will greatly affect the value of any U.S. missile shield. The U.S.S.R.'s options range from implacable hostility to guarded cooperation. If the United States decides to build a strategic shield, Soviet planners could go all out to defeat it by building more offensive weapons, antisatellite space mines, and other countermeasures. Or they could decide to move with the United States toward a world where defenses play a large role in the superpower relationship.

Protecting their nation against nuclear weapons is something the Soviets have worked on for a long time. The U.S.S.R. is blanketed with defenses against enemy bombers. A crude ABM system now stands guard around Moscow. A Soviet version of the U.S. SDI has long probed the utility of such exotic defensive weapons as lasers.

Reagan Administration officials in fact charge that the Soviet

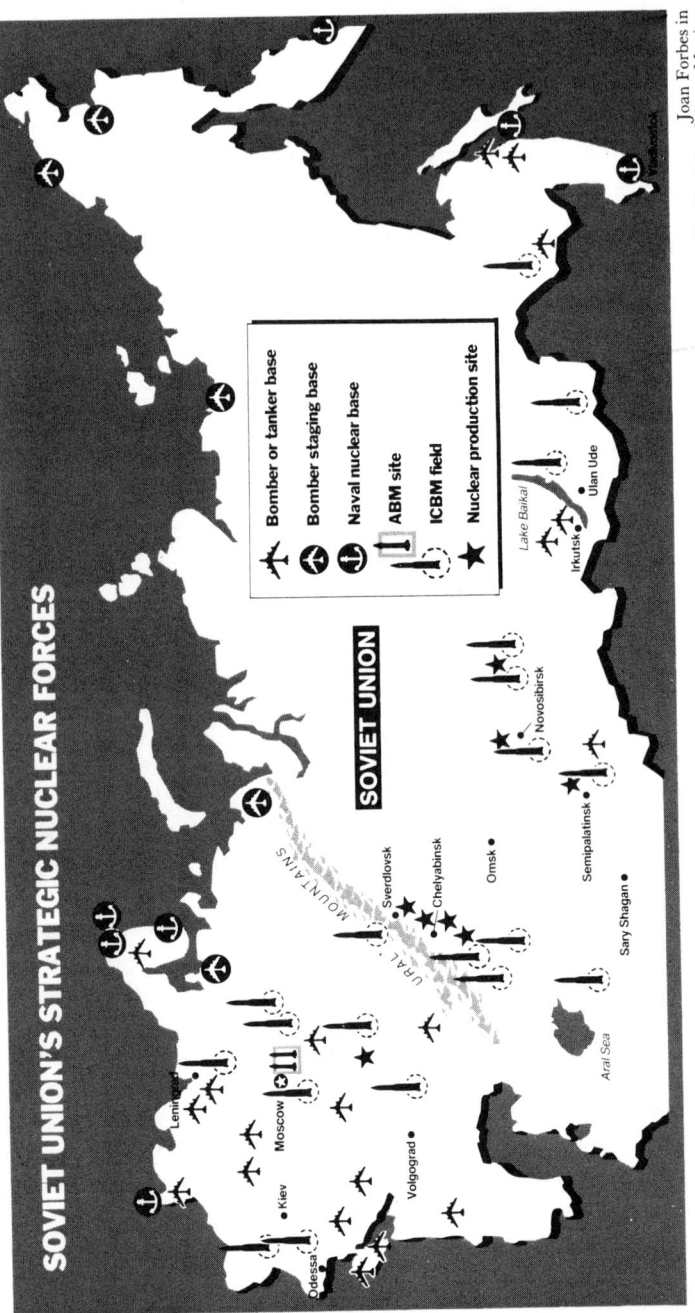

Union is preparing to forge ahead on its own and erect some sort of nationwide defense against nuclear missiles. But it seems clear that the Soviet space-shield program, while extensive, is in important ways inferior to its U.S. counterpart.

"Our technology base upon which SDI rests is sufficiently far ahead of the Soviets that I would say we are certainly exploiting our edge here," says Mr. Keyworth, science adviser to President Reagan.

Why should Americans care about the Soviet response to SDI? Unlike today, when superpowers hold each other hostage with vast nuclear arsenals, wouldn't a working space shield allow the United States to control its own destiny?

First, Soviet actions could well determine whether a U.S. missile defense is feasible at all. The quality of Soviet countermeasures would have a large effect on whether strategic defenses can be made tough enough to survive at a reasonable price—and SDI officials insist that a defense would have to be both survivable and cost-effective to be deployed.

Second, a missile shield could not be thrown up in a day like wallpaper; Soviet actions could make the world a more dangerous place during the time between a U.S. decision to build defenses and actual deployment. The U.S.S.R. could quickly build hundreds of new nuclear missiles and warheads before a U.S. space shield was in place, perhaps unnerving Western publics and providing an opportunity for the Soviets to force political concessions from the West.

And even if the United States and the U.S.S.R. decide that strategic defenses are worth pursuing, their moves toward a defense-dominated world would have to be carefully coordinated, like those of two men stepping into a canoe at once. Otherwise, either country might feel itself falling dangerously behind the other, greatly heightening world tensions.

Joint deployment would be much less tricky if it were scripted "in advance by explicit agreement between the United States and the Soviet Union," points out a recent Congressional Office of Technology Assessment report.

Overwhelming a Defensive System

The Soviet Union's initial response to a U.S. missile shield could well be to look for ways to overwhelm it. They might stack up new offensive weapons. They could do this relatively easily by churning out extra warheads for existing missiles.

The U.S.S.R.'s large SS-18 booster is today limited by arms agreements to a cargo of 10 warheads, but it is capable of carrying at least 18. Larger forces of cruise missiles and bombers might also be built, in an effort to skirt under a U.S. space-based shield.

Attempting to fool the defense is another Soviet option. Missiles could carry inexpensive Mylar balloon decoys, as well as warheads. Warheads could be concealed inside balloons, to make the defense's spotting problems even more difficult. Armor might be tried, too: Coating missile boosters with some sort of extra protective layer could make them resistant to attack by lasers or other directed-energy weapons.

Perhaps one of the most effective countermeasures the Soviets could use would be fast-burn missiles, which would finish their flaming boost stage inside Earth's atmosphere in a short 150 seconds. Fast-burn missiles would be safe from neutral particle-beam weapons and X-ray lasers, which cannot penetrate air well; and there would not be much time for the defense to attack them at all before they released their warheads.

Perfecting a fleet of fast-burn missiles would, however, take many years and millions of rubles.

Possible Soviet countermeasures are being studied very seriously, says Dr. Yonas, and a U.S. defensive system might well anticipate and handle them.

For example, one SDI concept calls for using pellets and artificial clouds of gas in space. Like Earth's atmosphere, the gas would strip away the lighter decoys, such as balloons, from a group of warheads. The pellets would actually shred the decoys.

Moscow might also simply try to destroy a U.S. missile shield at the start of hostilities. Space mines, which blow up near satellites, could be developed. According to the latest edition of the Pentagon's *Soviet Military Power,* the U.S.S.R. could have ground-based laser antisatellite (ASAT) weapons by the end of the 1980s; a Soviet ASAT using less-exotic technology has already been deployed.

SDI officials admit that ensuring survivability of a missile defense is one of their hardest challenges.

A shield's toughness will depend on the physical protection of armor and self-defense weapons; tactics, such as evasion by maneuverable satellites; and national policies, "agreements we might have with the Soviets in terms of how we operate in space," says Dr. Lorenzini, head of SDI's in-house architecture study.

Critics often contend that one result of Mr. Reagan's push for missile defense will be a militarization of the heavens, which have heretofore been a relative sanctuary from humanity's clashes on Earth.

But with military reconnaissance satellites already coasting through space and ASAT weapons in both the U.S. and Soviet arsenals, this militarization has in fact already happened, many Pentagon officers say.

"Clearly, most people would say in a better and decent world it would be nice if we could keep space pure and pristine. I don't think it's responsible for the [U.S.] Department of Defense to take such an altruistic point of view," says Air Force Colonel Hess, director of the SDI key technologies section.

Soviet Emphasis on Strategic Defense

Ironically, since the dawn of the nuclear age it has usually been the Soviet Union, not the United States, which stressed defense against nuclear weapons. Today Moscow complains bitterly about the U.S. SDI program; in 1967, Soviet Premier Alexei Kosygin said, "I think that a defensive system which prevents attack is not a cause of the arms race."

Thus it is possible that the Soviets could work on countermeasures against a U.S. shield while improving their own strategic defenses.

The Soviet Union today maintains a large force of traditional air defense weapons intended to protect against U.S. bombers and cruise missiles. According to the Pentagon, the Soviets have 1,200 interceptor aircraft and 1,200 surface-to-air missile sites dedicated to air defense missions.

This screen does not cause that much worry in the U.S. Air Force. The Strategic Air Command predicts that for the foreseeable future a high percentage of American bombers would be able to reach their targets. Years ago, Pentagon planners decided that in today's ballistic missile age defending the United States against bombers isn't worth that much effort. There are approximately 300 U.S.-based fighter aircraft dedicated to strategic defense.

As Reagan Administration officials are fond of pointing out, the U.S.S.R. also has the world's only working ABM system, deployed around Moscow.

Under the terms of the 1972 ABM Treaty, both the United States and the Soviet Union have the right to erect one such small defense. The United States built one around a ballistic-missile field in North Dakota, but soon scrapped it as costly and ineffective.

The Kremlin is currently upgrading Moscow's ballistic-missile defense. Fast nuclear-tipped SH-04 and SH-08 rockets are replacing sluggish Galosh interceptor missiles, the system's old standbys.

Still, "the upgraded Moscow system would be ineffective against a determined American strategic strike," judges Stanford University arms control expert David Holloway. "But it could provide some defense against theater [nuclear missile] systems such as the Pershing II," he adds.

The Soviets are also developing new radar that could enhance their early-warning and missile-tracking capabilities. This includes a large phased-array radar near Krasnoyarsk, in Siberia, that U.S. officials argue violates the ABM Treaty. The Soviets are also adding new mobile air-defense radars, which some analysts say may be able to perform missile-defense duties as well.

Then there is Soviet research into exotic defense technologies, their version of the U.S. SDI. A recent Pentagon study says the U.S.S.R. is devoting far more plant space, capital, and manpower to such projects than is the United States.

But while broader than its American counterpart, Soviet work in defense technology may still not be more productive.

"They are spending five to ten times as much on agriculture as we are, but I don't think anybody is maintaining there is a grain gap," says Mr. Pike of the Federation of American Scientists.

The Soviets have long been interested in directed-energy weapons, destructive rays that might form part of an advanced screen against incoming ballistic missiles.

Some 10,000 Soviet scientists and half a dozen research facilities are thought to be working on high-energy lasers, for instance.

Soviet laser work may have moved beyond basic research to the development of prototype weapons. At Sary Shagan, a missile range in Soviet Central Asia where some of the most advanced research is under way, there are now two lasers that could "blind" low-orbiting U.S. satellites, charge Pentagon officials.

If the Soviets skip some testing, the U.S. Defense Department estimates that they could deploy an Earth-based laser shield against missiles in 10 years, ahead of the SDI timetable. The Soviets might well choose to do this: Several times in the past they have prematurely deployed new systems of marginal use in order to beat the United States.

The Central Intelligence Agency is a bit more skeptical of Moscow's prospects. In a report to the U.S. Congress in June, the CIA predicted that the U.S.S.R. could not deploy a missile-defense system until after the turn of the century.

Like the United States, the Soviets have also long been interested in two other exotic technologies: particle beams and radio-frequency beams. Particle beams—streams of atoms or subatomic particles—are considered mainly useful for attacking targets in space. Radio-frequency beams, which use microwaves, hold potential for destroying the electronics of a missile or satellite. The Soviets hold an edge over the United States in both technologies, according to U.S. intelligence officials, but still have far to go before they can make actual particle-beam and radio-frequency weapons.

A broad shield against missiles, particularly one with some

components in space, needs more than weapons. It also requires sensors to spot targets, secure communications links, and computers to run the battle.

SDI officials say progress in these miscellaneous technologies may make or break any missile shield, and in these areas the Soviet Union is probably far behind the United States.

Writing reliable computer software to run a missile shield, for instance, is today far beyond the capability of U.S. engineers. And Soviet computer technology is at least a generation cruder than its U.S. counterpart.

"I don't care how big a laser they can build," says Stephen M. Meyer, a Soviet defense specialist at MIT. "If they aren't capable of pointing it at anything, who cares?"

Still, the Pentagon claims that the scope of the Soviets' strategic defensive programs suggests they may be preparing to burst the limits of the 1972 ABM Treaty and erect a nationwide missile defense.

At the very least, Pentagon officials say, Moscow's work on upgrading radars and surface-to-air missile sites means it is better positioned than the United States to build a relatively crude shield, using off-the-shelf technology, in the next decade or so.

"It would really give us fits if they did," says one Pentagon official.

If the Soviet Union raced ahead with its own defense, while bolstering its offensive arsenal, Kremlin planners might come to believe they had strategic superiority and could attack the United States, or threaten to attack it, without fear of retaliation.

Thus Pentagon officials from Defense Secretary Weinberger on down argue that the U.S. SDI is really not an initiative at all, but a response to Soviet actions.

Critics of the U.S. program argue that this view of the Soviets exaggerates their capabilities.

Kremlin officials are not about to order a "breakout" from the ABM Treaty, because they know that doing so would be like "throwing gasoline" on the American SDI effort, says one defense analyst.

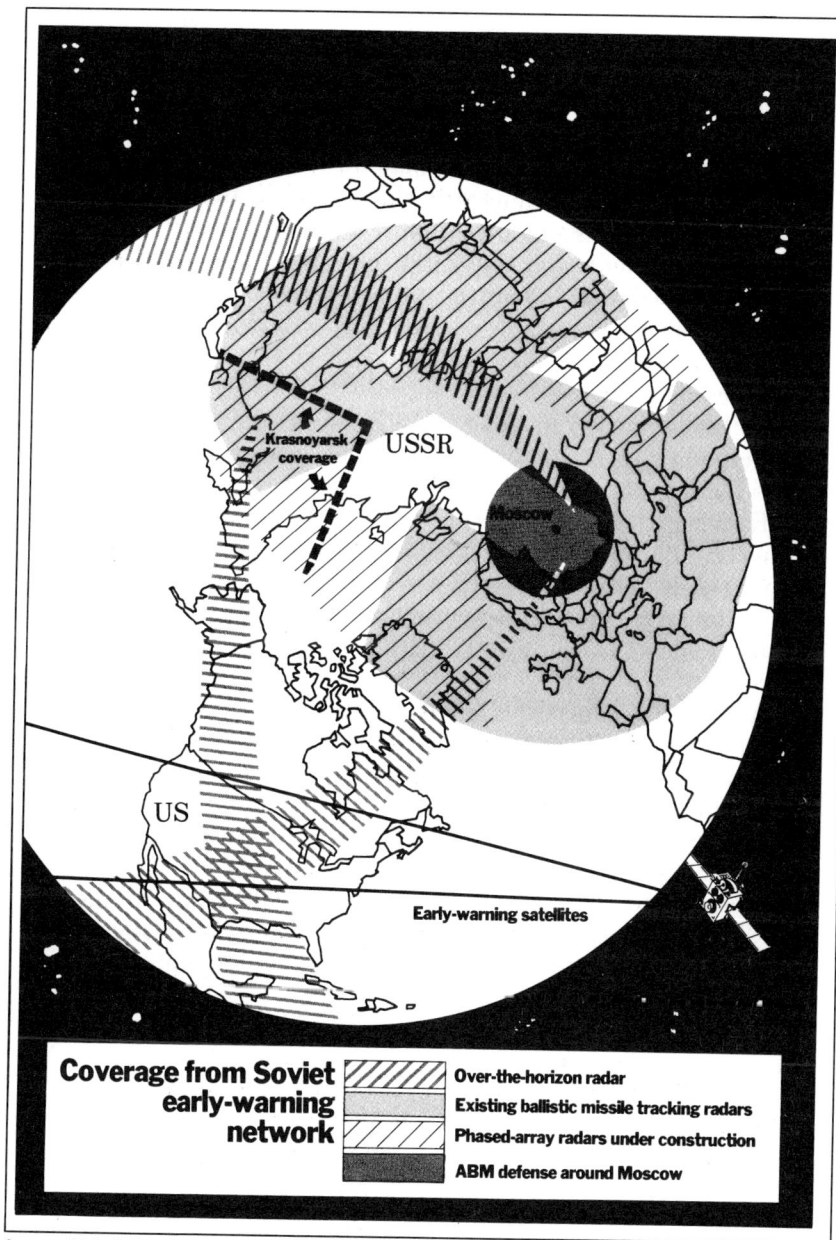

Source: U.S. Defense Department

Robin Jareaux in *The Christian Science Monitor*
© 1985 TCSPS.

A Very Tricky Transition Period

Critics also are concerned about SDI's effect on superpower stability. Here they turn the Pentagon's argument around: If it would destabilize the nuclear balance for the U.S.S.R. to deploy defenses ahead of the United States, wouldn't it also be destabilizing for the United States to erect defenses before the U.S.S.R.?

The transition from today's strategic situation, where superpowers rely solely on offensive arsenals, to the world of strategic defense would be a very delicate dance—even according to SDI officials. Few people say the United States could just build defenses on its own.

"I think if we've convinced ourselves this is the way to go, the Soviets will have convinced themselves this is the way to go, too," says Dr. Yonas.

Each step toward defenses by both sides would have to be made gingerly to keep the other fellow from feeling he was becoming dangerously vulnerable by being left behind.

Many experts inside and outside government feel this transition period would have to be planned in advance by a superpower agreement.

A necessary part of this agreement, these experts say, will be strict limits on offensive arms. Otherwise, defenses might not be effective enough to make sense, or cheap enough to afford. "In my view offensive restraints are necessary," says Dr. Coll.

Other officials argue that offensive arms cuts will in fact follow, not precede, deployment of defenses: As defenses are gradually strengthened, both sides will see their nuclear weapons becoming less and less useful, and will become amenable to greater and greater reductions in their arsenals. The arms spiral will go down, instead of up.

"Defensive technology is the enabling mechanism that will make this chemistry of arms reduction work," Dr. Yonas argues.

If strategic defenses turn out to be feasible, will the Soviets really agree to go along? That is difficult for Westerners to predict—it is not for nothing that Winston Churchill called the Soviet Union "a riddle wrapped in a mystery inside an enigma."

It is clear that the Soviets are working on defenses. But in the near term, most observers don't expect the Soviet Union to radically accelerate its military programs, offensive or defensive, in response to SDI.

For one thing, too many political and technical uncertainties surround the nascent program. In addition, the Kremlin wouldn't find it easy to divert resources from other sectors of the economy—many of which lag their Western counterparts.

"They can't afford to plow forward with an SDI on the American scale," says Jonathan Haslam, a Soviet specialist at Johns Hopkins School of Advanced International Studies in Washington, D.C.

But the very fact that SDI exists has already changed the superpower relationship, helping bring Moscow back to the arms-bargaining table, while at the same time making those talks more complicated. The issue of defenses, which has now gone very public in the West, is likely to affect superpower relations for some time to come.

Writes MIT's Dr. Meyer in *Survival,* the journal of the International Institute for Strategic Studies in London: "For the Soviet Union, the U.S. SDI program is quickly becoming symbolic of a more fundamental challenge between states, . . . calling into contention the political, economic and industrial, scientific and technological, and military potentials of the superpowers."

The Politics of Space

In the U.S. Capitol, a roomful of conservatives is cheering for missile defense, over dessert. "I'm for an arms race—in defensive systems!" cries activist Phyllis Schlafly. A block away, at 100 Maryland Avenue, liberal lobbyists meet every Thursday and plot against President Reagan's ballistic-missile defense initiative. "It's so big, we can't stop it. But we have to slow it down," says a participant in the meetings. In Washington, a political fight is heating up over the President's proposed nuclear-missile shield.

The immediate battles will be over money for SDI. But both sides know something far more fundamental is at stake: whether the United States will reverse its nuclear strategy of the last 20 years and erect any sort of missile defense.

SDI, after all, is an ambitious package, involving billions of dollars for research on lasers, high-speed electric cannons, and other exotic weapons. Its stated goal is to see if an effective shield that eventually makes nuclear weapons unusable is possible.

Congress could reject SDI totally, embrace it, or simply redirect the program's broad approach. Members of Congress might vote to protect U.S. intercontinental missile bases, for instance, with rings of rocket interceptors. They could decide to defend a mixture of some missile bases and cities.

"There may be something there," muses Representative Les Aspin (D-Wis.), influential chairman of the House Armed Services Committee.

The conservatives crammed into a Capitol room last September represent one pole of this debate.

They had gathered for a meeting of the Coalition for the Strategic Defense Initiative, a lobbying group whose members include the Moral Majority and Citizens for Reagan.

A series of speakers thumped home the message that America needs a shield against Soviet missiles—a broad effective shield, not just a demure little defense around Minuteman missile bases. Besides Phyllis Schlafly, longtime spokeswoman for conservative causes, hosts included Representative Jack Kemp (R-N.Y.) ("Whenever anyone asks, I say I'm a dove—a heavily armed dove") and Senator Malcolm Wallop (R-Wyo.), a laser-weapons champion who complained that the Pentagon is not pursuing missile defense with sufficient skill.

Underlying all the speeches, punctuated with the constant clatter of silverware, was the theme that the Soviets cannot be trusted, that defense and not arms treaties is the way to true security. Thus the coalition's purpose is to "raise public awareness" in support of SDI and perhaps to save SDI from itself.

The liberal lobbyists and their weekly meetings illustrate the other pole of the strategic-defense argument. Every Thursday at 1:00 p.m., representatives from the Union of Concerned Scientists, the Council for a Livable World, and other self-styled peace groups meet to coordinate their anti-SDI tactics. This ad-hoc committee has dubbed itself the Space Policy Working Group.

For the most part, its members believe that new weapons systems are dangerous because they goad the Soviets into building new systems of their own. This, they say, leaves both nations in the same strategic situation—but poorer. They feel arms control agreements, not new technology, represent real protection.

Missile defense "is not going to end the arms race," says Union of Concerned Scientists lobbyist Charles Monfort. "You'd still spend billions on countermeasures, and counter-countermeasures."

Congress Caught in the Middle

Caught between these opposing camps, but so far paying little attention to either, is the U.S. Congress. Though legislators have sawed the occasional hunk out of SDI's budget, they have done nothing to change the fundamental thrust of the program.

The SDI, after all, is just the sort of thing that Congress has trouble understanding. It's big and it's highly technical. That's a problem in the Capitol, which is swarming with lawyers, not physicists.

"Congress's knowledge of technology? It's abysmally poor," says Senator John Glenn (D-Ohio).

Senator Glenn, a former astronaut, says colleagues often ask his opinion of SDI. After several grand tours of U.S. missile defense labs, he says the experiments are impressive, but he's not sure when or if a working system could be built. "This program is mind-boggling," he says.

Another reason Congress has yet to focus fully on SDI is that congressmen have been fixated on another strategic-weapons acronymn: MX.

The MX missile was first proposed by the Pentagon more than a decade ago. Larger and more accurate than the venerable Minuteman, the MX was supposed to strengthen U.S. land-based nuclear forces.

But Congress and the Pentagon kept arguing about where this wonder weapon was to be kept—in silos clustered close together, on trains shuttling around vast tracts of land.

The argument went on so long that the MX became less proposed hardware and more a preeminent symbol of nuclear policy. Members had little attention for other strategic issues. But this year Congress voted to deploy 50 MXs in old Minuteman silos, and the issue appears closed.

"Many of the groups involved in the MX battle are now shifting to star wars," points out Kathleen Sheekey, a lobbyist for Common Cause, a public-interest lobby group.

"What if we get this thing designed and built and then they just use it as a bargaining chip?"

Thus the SDI is entering a crucial period. In Geneva, it is one of the subjects on the table in arms control talks between the United States and the Soviet Union. In Washington, it is beginning to gain prominence as an issue in Congress.

"The next year is going to be pivotal for SDI," says an aide to Senator Pete Wilson (R-Calif.), who supports the program.

There is no chance that Congress will soon kill the program. Among members there is a consensus that the United States should have some sort of missile-defense research.

The question—as is often the case on Capitol Hill—will come down to money: Should SDI receive $26 billion over the next five years, as the Reagan Administration has requested?

This year legislators waved their shears over the SDI budget and proclaimed victory. In an authorizing bill, $900 million was trimmed from SDI's 1986 budget request. But the $2.75 billion that remained represented an increase of almost 100 percent over the 1985 budget.

Future SDI budget battles are likely to center on what the money goes for, as much as its absolute level. In particular, critics worry that SDI, as it is now shaped, will eventually stretch or break the terms of the 1972 ABM Treaty.

At issue here is the legality of 15 big experiments SDI plans to hold through the early 1990s. The ABM Treaty has traditionally been interpreted as banning "development" of "components" for other than land-based ABM systems, and critics contend some SDI demonstrations may violate this restriction. The Pentagon says the rest are allowable lab research, or involve "subcomponents," not "components."

"It's a rather ambiguous situation," says Representative George Brown (D-Calif.), who complains that the Pentagon has simply "defined away the problem."

So look for continued efforts in Congress to cut funds for major SDI tests. The Pentagon, for its part, is not just waiting to be cornered on this question: Officials recently floated a new interpretation of the ABM Treaty, saying it allows for the development of "exotic technologies."

To a certain extent, fights over treaty language and budget lines are so much dancing on the head of a Minuteman.

Focused on these narrow issues, SDI critics and supporters alike can forget the larger vision that Mr. Reagan held before the U.S. public, and the political effect that vision has already had.

In calling for a world where nuclear weapons are "impotent and obsolete," the President employed the sort of Utopian rhetoric associated with theologians and antinuclear activists, not politicians. Whatever the merits of the SDI program, President Reagan's words alone have given him a moral sheen in voters' eyes, as even some critics say.

"The arms control and peace communities were taken by surprise. The President has grabbed the moral high ground, somewhat," says James Wetekam, a lobbyist for the United Church of Christ Office for Church in Society.

Mr. Wetekam, part of the anti-SDI coalition of lobbyists, says

Mr. Reagan has "been effective to some extent" in capturing public opinion for missile defense. Capitol Hill committee staff members of all political persuasions generally agree.

Public Opinion: Few Clear Themes

Public opinion polls on the issue, however, show few clear themes. A recent roundup of star-wars surveys in *Public Opinion* magazine, published by the American Enterprise Institute, concludes that "responses bounce all over, depending on which nerve the pollsters touch."

Such movement, said the magazine, is typical when an issue is complicated and the public not well informed.

In general, the polls cited in the roundup show more people favor development of a star-wars system than oppose it.

Opinions on what the system would actually do, however, skitter around like a cat on ice skates. Only one poll, a CBS News/New York Times effort, asked simply whether missile defense would work; 62 percent of respondents said that it could.

Building and keeping public support for missile defense is both necessary and difficult, admit Administration officials.

The recognition of this fact has led pro- and anti-SDI groups outside the government to begin multimedia ad campaigns to try to build support for their positions.

"No one is going to write us a blank check and say, 'Go, come back in 15 years and build us something,'" says Dr. Yonas. To keep voters and Congress satisfied, SDI in the next few years will have to produce technical achievements that are the stuff of press releases, he adds.

SDI won't be able to produce these advances on its own. It will need help from defense-contractor friends. Such friends should not be hard to make, given that missile defense could be the biggest thing to hit the arms industry since the cost-plus contract.

SDI right now is just a research program, and thus still small change compared to such things as building Trident submarines. Boeing Aerospace is currently the No. 1 SDI contractor, with $130 million worth of business.

But if a missile shield ever goes into production, it would mean immense amounts of business—rough estimates are that a full system would cost at least $800 billion.

Companies are thus elbowing each other in a race to become SDI favorites.

Ten contracts to study missile-defense architectures, let last year, were among the most hotly contested in Pentagon history. With contracts for such big programs as the B-1 and Stealth bombers basically awarded, companies are looking at SDI as the last mother lode of untapped defense spending this century, one industry official says.

"SDI offers you the chance to get in on the ground floor of something really big," says Walter Edgington, GTE marketing vice-president.

Critics worry that this promise of money will make missile defense a pork barrel of the heavens, supported by Congress because of the jobs it provides, not because of its intrinsic virtue.

Seventy-seven percent of SDI research money has flowed to the districts of congressmen who sit on the key Armed Services or Appropriations Committees, according to an analysis released earlier this year by the Council on Economic Priorities.

But Mr. Reagan's words for missile defense have done more than argue morality and make corporate hearts beat faster.

They have also launched a broad debate among university professors, think-tank scholars, and once and future government officials whose careers involve thinking about nuclear weapons. This debate is not so much about the President's vision as it is about whether a missile defense—however leaky—would be a good thing.

Arguments for Strategic Defense

In concrete terms this means Congress could reject SDI's crash-program style and broad emphasis, yet still embrace the idea that defensive weapons could be a useful addition to America's offensive nuclear arsenal.

A recent report from the Congressional Office of Technology

Assessment identified four possible levels of defenses, from limited protection for U.S. military forces to an extremely capable shield.

Those in favor of defensive weapons usually begin their argument from the premise that U.S. land-based nuclear missiles and control centers are dangerously vulnerable to Soviet attack. Furthermore, they add, U.S. voters may grow faint in the face of today's assured nuclear destruction, and refuse to pay for new nuclear swords. "Democratic publics will sooner or later retreat to pacifism and unilateral disarmament," writes former Secretary of State Henry A. Kissinger.

Defensive weapons could be a politically attractive way to protect U.S. forces, advocates say. If this is beginning to sound like a rerun from the 1960s, it is: The argument is similar to that put forward two decades ago when the United States debated but did not build more than a token ABM force. The difference in the 1980s is that modern technology would enable an ABM system to actually work, according to proponents.

Light, mobile defender rockets could be shifted from base to base, in a sort of nuclear poker with the U.S.S.R. Soviet military planners could never be sure what defensive forces were where, and therefore could never be sure a surprise nuclear strike would succeed, no matter what their offensive strength, and therefore would never launch first.

"Defenses do not have to be nearly leakproof to be useful in deterring Soviet attack," concludes Fred S. Hoffman, nuclear theorist and head of a 1983 presidential study of the strategic implications of missile defense.

Critics reply, first of all, that the case for limited strategic defense is based on the mistaken premise of U.S. weakness. While U.S. land-based missiles may theoretically be vulnerable to their Soviet counterparts, say critics, U.S. submarines are not. A single Trident sub has enough nuclear missiles to devastate vast tracts of the U.S.S.R.; while such firepower cruises safely beneath the seas, only a madman would launch a nuclear strike against the United States, claim missile-defense critics.

"A threat to the U.S. retaliatory capability does not exist today and is not likely to arise during this century," writes former Secretary of Defense Harold Brown.

Second, some critics complain that limited missile defenses would actually make the world a more dangerous place, because they would inflame Soviet distrust.

"Why? Because a leaky umbrella offers no protection in a downpour but is quite useful in a drizzle," says former Defense Secretary McNamara. In other words, a small-scale missile defense could not cope with an all-out Soviet attack. But if the United States hit the U.S.S.R. with a first strike, limited defenses could mop up the ragged Soviet retaliation.

Kremlin leaders, who suspect that the United States yearns to once again be the world's supreme nuclear power, might thus respond to U.S. defenses with provocative moves of their own—perhaps an all-out offensive arms buildup, says Mr. McNamara.

Central Security Issue in Congress

Work on limited defenses and an SDI-type full-dress program are not mutually exclusive. Differences involve timing and emphasis. SDI officials see limited systems as the first step toward bigger things; small-scale-defense advocates see SDI as a Cecil B. DeMille production that could stand budget cuts.

What seems clear is that this multifaceted debate—big defense versus small defense versus no defense at all—is becoming the central security issue in Congress, if not the whole Western alliance. Its prominence alone has changed the superpowers' relationship. It may distract the United States from other matters worthy of attention. "People always want to talk about SDI," grumbles Dr. Freeman Dyson, physicist and author of two acclaimed books on nuclear weapons. "The Soviet offer of a comprehensive test-ban treaty, getting the North Atlantic Treaty Organization to adopt a 'no first use' nuclear strategy—those things are a hundred times more important than SDI."

Talking It Over

A Note for Students and Discussion Groups

This issue of the HEADLINE SERIES, like its predecessors, is published for every serious reader, specialized or not, who takes an interest in the subject. Many of our readers will be in classrooms, seminars or community discussion groups. Particularly with them in mind, we present below some discussion questions—suggested as a starting point only—and references for further reading.

Discussion Questions

Defense against nuclear attack is not a new concept, but President Reagan's strategic defense initiative differs considerably from earlier schemes. Describe the differences.

President Reagan sees the strategic defense initiative as an alternative to deterrence of nuclear war by threat of mutual assured destruction. Explain what he means and give your opinion of his views.

Few experts believe it will ever be possible to devise a fully "leakproof" strategic defense system. Do you think SDI research should nevertheless continue? Give the reasons for your conclusions.

The Soviet Union strongly opposes SDI. Should Americans be concerned about the Soviet response to SDI?

If the United States deploys a ballistic missile defense system, how do you think the Soviets will respond? In your opinion, how would deployment affect the prospects for arms control?

READING LIST

Achieving Effective Arms Control: Recommendations, Background and Analysis. Report of the Committee on International Arms Control and Security Affairs of the Association of the Bar of the City of New York, 1985. Available at $5.00 from the Association of the Bar of the City of New York, 42 West 44th St., New York, N.Y. 10036. Starting from the premise that decisions on missile defense systems will be pivotal to the future success or failure of arms control, the report includes background on the current status of arms control, a pro and con discussion of SDI, and a concluding chapter with recommendations.

Bethe, Hans A., Garwin, Richard L., Gottfried, Kurt, and Kendall, Henry W., "Space-based Ballistic Missile Defense." *Scientific American,* October 1984. Union of Concerned Scientists' objections to SDI, based on 1983–84 studies.

Bundy, McGeorge, Kennan, George F., McNamara, Robert S., and Smith, Gerard, "The President's Choice: Star Wars or Arms Control." *Foreign Affairs,* Winter 1984/85. Four former officials with defense expertise argue that SDI violates the ABM Treaty and will kill arms control.

Drell, Sidney D., Farley, Philip J., and Holloway, David, *The Reagan Strategic Defense Initiative: A Technical, Political and Arms Control Assessment.* Cambridge, Mass., Ballinger Publishing Co., 1985. The authors have "grave doubts, on technical and strategic grounds, that substantial acceleration or expansion of ABM research and development is warranted or prudent."

Jastrow, Robert, "The War Against 'Star Wars.'" *Commentary*, December 1984. Former NASA official rebuts Union of Concerned Scientists' criticisms of SDI.

Krepon, Michael, "Arms Control Verification and Compliance." HEADLINE SERIES No. 270. New York, Foreign Policy Association, September/October 1984. Overview of the difficulties of assuring compliance with arms control agreements.

Payne, Keith B., and Gray, Colin S., "Nuclear Policy and the Defensive Transition." *Foreign Affairs*, Spring 1984. The case for SDI by two experts at the National Institute for Public Policy.

"The President's Strategic Defense Initiative." *Department of State Bulletin*, March 1985. Sets forth the Administration position on SDI, including a section refuting common criticisms of the program. Foreword by the President.

Schlesinger, James R., "Rhetoric and Realities in the Star Wars Debate." *International Security*, Summer 1985. Former secretary of defense argues that the United States should limit defensive technologies in return for limits on Soviet offensive forces.

Sedacca, Sandra, and DeGrasse, Robert, *Star Wars: Questions and Answers on the Space Weapons Debate.* Washington, D.C., Common Cause, 1985. A layman's guide to SDI.

Sloan, Stanley R., and Gray, Robert C., "Nuclear Strategy and Arms Control: Challenges for U.S. Policy." HEADLINE SERIES No. 261. New York, Foreign Policy Association, November/December 1982. Analyzes the challenges facing U.S. policymakers in attempting to defend the United States and its allies and to control the nuclear arms race.

"'Star Wars' and the Geneva Talks: What Future for Arms Control?" *Great Decisions '86.* New York, Foreign Policy Association, 1986.

The star-wars debate has stalled arms control talks. Article discusses whether the United States should trade SDI for an agreement or speed its development.

"Weapons in Space." *Daedalus,* Spring 1985, Vol. I, Concepts and Technology; Summer 1985, Vol. II, Implications for Security. Two full-issue compilations of short essays on various aspects of the space weapons controversy.

This is one of a number of issues of the HEADLINE SERIES, *dealing with arms control and security issues whose publication is being supported by the John D. and Catherine T. MacArthur Foundation.*

Since 1918, the Foreign Policy Association has worked to help Americans gain a better understanding of problems in U.S. foreign policy and to stimulate informed citizen discussion of, and participation in, world affairs.

The Association is independent and nonpartisan, has no affiliation with government and takes no position on questions under debate. Rather, it seeks to call attention to, and to clarify opposing views on, those foreign policy issues which government and people must resolve in democratic partnership.

FPA's publications, in addition to the year-round HEADLINE SERIES, *include the annual* Great Decisions, *a briefing and discussion guide on eight current foreign policy topics. Reports on the annual* Great Decisions *"Opinion Ballots" are a valued index to the foreign policy views of informed citizens. Both directly and through the media support they receive, FPA publications reach out to more students, libraries, citizens and community groups than any other world affairs educational service today.*

FPA provides an open world affairs meeting service to the New York and Washington communities. Throughout the year, FPA's podium, with the opportunity of audience discussion, is offered to leaders, experts and institutions concerned with, and taking varying positions on, current issues of U.S. foreign policy.

By such means, FPA seeks to achieve what Elihu Root emphasized in the early years of the Association's existence:

> "The control of foreign relations by modern democracies creates a new and pressing demand for popular education in international affairs."

Foreign Policy Association
Editorial Advisory Committee

Chairman:
  Stanley H. Hoffmann
    Douglas Dillon Professor of the Civilization of France
    Chairman, Center for European Studies, Harvard University

Members:
  Carol Edler Baumann
    Director, International Studies and Programs
    University of Wisconsin-Milwaukee
  Earl W. Foell
    Editor in Chief
    The Christian Science Monitor
  John Lewis Gaddis
    Professor of History
    Ohio University
  Edwin Newman
    Columnist
    King Features Syndicate
  Ponchitta Pierce
    Host and Co-producer
    "Today in New York," WNBC-TV
  Andrew F. Smith
    President
    Global Perspectives in Education
  James A. Van Fleet
    Executive Director, International Center
    University of Louisville
  Samuel S. Vaughan
    Senior Vice-President
    Random House
  Leo M. Weins
    President
    The H. W. Wilson Company
  Allen Weinstein
    President
    The Center for Democracy

FPA Editor:
  Nancy L. Hoepli

FPA's Editorial Advisory Committee was formed to give the Association's publishing program the benefit of a wide range of talent in journalism, broadcasting, education, community service and business. Topics, approaches, authors, and audiences to be served by future FPA publications are discussed by the Committee and FPA's editors at their meetings.